Meeting the True Dragon

Zen Master Dogen's *Fukanzazengi*

Meeting the True Dragon

Zen Master Dogen's *Fukanzazengi*

Commentary by Daniel Gallagher

Forward by Catherine Genno Pagès Roshi

Hope Street Press
Liverpool & Naples

Meeting the True Dragon

Copyright © 2019 Daniel Gallagher

All rights reserved.

No part of this book may be reproduced or used in any manner whatsoever without the express written permission of the publisher except as permitted by United States copyright law. No part of this book may be stored in a retrieval system or transmitted in any form or by any means including electronic, electrostatic, magnetic tape, mechanical, photocopying, recording or otherwise without the prior permission in writing of the publisher.

The translation of the *Fukanzazengi* reprinted in this book is copyright © 1973 by The Eastern Buddhist Society, Norman Waddell and Masao Abe, translators. It first appeared in "The Eastern Buddhist," Vol. 6, No. 2. Reprinted here with grateful acknowledgment.

First edition December 2019

ISBN: 979-8-9915155-1-1

Cover design: German Creative

Hope Street Press
Liverpool & Naples

This commentary is dedicated with love to:

Catherine Genno Pagès Roshi

who first introduced me to the true dragon.

*Please, honored followers of Zen,
long accustomed to groping for the elephant,
do not be suspicious of the true dragon.*

– Eihei Dogen

Table of Contents

Foreword..i

Preface..iii

Introduction..1

Fukanzazengi...11

Commentary..17

Acknowledgements..81

Works Cited...83

Foreword

This commentary on the *Fukanzazengi* was written by a longtime practitioner of Zen, a lover of the Dharma and someone who is deeply devoted to meditation. After having thoroughly examined this text in the very intimate setting of numerous private interviews with a teacher, Daniel Gallagher meditated with each line, allowing the *Fukanzazengi* to resonate within him. This approach to becoming intimate with a text allows the written words from ancient masters to penetrate us deeply and nourish our own innate longing for awakening, allowing our own treasure-store to open of itself. Love and compassion can then emerge and help us to manifest the Buddha Way in our everyday life.

Before starting his spiritual quest which would take him to China and back to Japan, Dogen Zenji went through a period of "great doubt," triggered by the Mahayana teaching that all beings are endowed with Buddha Nature, an intrinsic enlightened nature which is present in every one of us. The burning question that Dogen Zenji had was: *if all beings intrinsically have Buddha Nature, then what need is there for practice?*

Dogen Zenji wrote the *Fukanzazengi* immediately upon his return to Japan from China where he had spent several years practicing intensely under the guidance of his teacher Ruijing. It was with Ruijing that Dogen had a powerful experience of "dropping off body and mind." Finally, practice and realization were one – the "great doubt" had been taken care of. We do not practice in order to become enlightened; we practice as an expression of our enlightened nature. This is a text for practitioners who want to go beyond theories, concepts and intellectual understanding.

May we all be inspired by this commentary and may it help us to let the echo of the *Fukanzazengi* resonate even more deeply within us in order to penetrate further into Dogen Zenji's practice-realization.

Catherine Genno Pagès Roshi
Montreuil

Preface

My interest in the *Fukanzazengi* began, in earnest, in 2018 during the three-month spring training period at Yokoji Zen Mountain Center in California. I had asked the abbott, Rev. Charles Tenshin Fletcher Roshi, if we could work on a text together whereby I would present each line during Dokusan.[1] Tenshin Roshi suggested that I take a look at Eihei Dogen's *Fukanzazengi*, which I had read before but never studied intimately. During the training period, on an almost daily basis, I presented my understanding of the *Fukanzazengi* line by line in Dokusan. I did not take any notes during these exchanges nor did I write anything down afterwards. I had no intention, in fact, of writing anything on the

---

[1] Private interview with a teacher.

Fukanzazengi. It wasn't until many months later when I was back in Cambridge, Massachusetts that I began to feel inhabited by Dogen's writing, to the point where I could think of little else. I found myself going back to the *Fukanzazengi* and rereading it, taking each line again while doing zazen.

This commentary, therefore, is the result of that process of doing zazen with the *Fukanzazengi* line by line, and then writing down whatever came up. It is my hope that this commentary will, at least in part, illuminate the inexpressible heart of Dogen's *Fukanzazengi*, and in doing so may it inspire others not only to develop an appreciation of Master Dogen's writing, but also to go deeper into their own spiritual practice as Dogen himself so often urges us to do.

Daniel Gallagher
Naples

Introduction

Eihei Dogen was born in the year 1200 in Kyoto, the ancient capital of Japan. Much of the historical facts of his childhood remain obscure since the only biography of Master Dogen wasn't written until the 15th century and even that remained unpublished for hundreds of years. According to legendary accounts, however, Dogen was born into an aristocratic family and was an intelligent and precocious child, raised in the Tendai school of Buddhism which was both popular and politically powerful in Japan at the time. We are told that his first spiritual awakening to the world of impermanence came at the age of seven at his mother's funeral when he saw smoke rising from a stick of incense. The loss of his mother, coming as it did on the heels of the loss of his father five years earlier, was particularly devastating to the young Dogen. At the age of 12 he was ordained in the Tendai school and lived on Mount Hiei at Enryakuji temple. A few years later the young Dogen left Enryakuji temple and went to study at Kenninji temple which happened to be the first Zen temple established in Japan. The facts concerning this move from one temple to another remain unclear.[2]

Dogen studied for many years at Kenninji with his teacher, Butsuju Myozen (1184 - 1225), from whom he received Rinzai transmission in the Oryu lineage.[3] Myozen was the only successor of Myoan Eisai (1141 – 1215) who had traveled to China and received transmission in the lineage of Master Rinzai. As such, he is credited with brining Rinzai Zen to Japan. It was here at Kenninji temple that Dogen had a thorough training in koan study and would first become a Zen teacher in the lineage of Master Rinzai. This koan study would go on to influence Dogen's writing for the rest of his life.

In 1223 Dogen's teacher Myozen decided to make a pilgrimage to China and invited his young student to go with him. They set sail from Japan to mainland China and spent many months on pilgrimage visiting one monastery after another with Dogen testing and honing his understanding with various Zen masters. In 1225

---

[2] For more information about Dogen's early life, see Loori, "Dropping Off Body and Mind." All footnote citations are listed in the "Works Cited" section of this book found on page 83.
[3] Today this Rinzai lineage exists only in the Soto school through Dogen. See: Kazuaki Tanahashi and John Daido Loori, p. xxiv.

both Myozen and Dogen arrived at Tiantong monastery where they decided to stay. In an unfortunate turn of events, Myozen died soon after their arrival, leaving Dogen alone in China.[4] Dogen thought very highly of the abbot of the monastery, Tiantong Rujing (1162 - 1228),[5] who deeply impressed Dogen with his understanding of the Dharma, his wisdom and his comportment. Dogen felt that he could deepen his understanding under the guidance of Rujing and decided to stay at Rujing's monastery. Rujing, however, was not in the Rinzai school of Zen as Myozen had been, but rather in the Caodong school, later to be known in Japan as the Soto school.

Rujing's style of Zen was thus different from that which Dogen had experienced under Myozen at Kenninji temple. Rujing was less concerned with koan practice and placed more emphasis on zazen, almost to the exclusion of everything else. He said to Dogen:

> Cross-legged sitting is the Dharma of ancient Buddhas. Practicing meditation is dropping off body and mind. Offering incense, doing prostrations, chanting Nembutsu, repentance and reading sutras are not essential; in just sitting it is fully accomplished.[6]

---

[4] When Dogen returned to Japan in 1227 he brought his late master's ashes with him.
[5] Tendo Nyojo in Japanese.
[6] Leighton, p. 386.

It was in this spirit that Dogen wholeheartedly threw himself into his practice. Although he had already had awakening experiences as a child as well as while studying with Myozen at Kenninji temple, his mind was still not fully put to rest. Dogen practiced zazen day and night, throwing caution to the wind, not worrying about fatigue or illness, claiming that to die of sickness among such fine monks would be a good thing. Then, early one morning at around three o'clock, Dogen was doing zazen in the dark meditation hall when suddenly he heard Rujing shout at a fellow monk: "When you study under a master you must drop body and mind! What's the use of single-minded intense sleeping!" When Dogen heard "you must drop off body and mind!" body and mind dropped off and all of Dogen's questions and doubts were instantly resolved.[7]

Dogen went to see Rujing who promptly confirmed his realization. That year, Dogen received transmission from Rujing, sanctioning him as a Zen teacher in his lineage. Rujing then instructed Dogen to return to Japan and begin teaching there, which Dogen did, arriving in Kyoto in 1227 and going directly to Kenninji temple where he and Myozen had practiced before.

In 1227, soon after his return to Kenninji, Master Dogen wrote what would eventually be called *Fukanzazengi*, often translated as *Universal Recommendation of Zazen for all People* or *Principles of Seated Meditation*. It was the first

---

[7] Loori, "Dropping Off Body and Mind."

known essay that Dogen wrote upon his return to Japan and although Dogen would go on to become one of the most prolific writers in Zen history, he would return to the *Fukanzazengi* to improve, clarify and expand upon it. It should be noted that the *Fukanzazengi*, written in Chinese, was largely based on a very popular Chinese text called *Tso-Ch'an I*, composed in 1103 and attributed to Ch'ang-lu Tsung-tse.

The *Tso-Ch'an I* is the earliest known work of its kind in so far as it promotes the benefits of zazen to everyone and gives precise instructions on how to meditate correctly. This was practically unheard of at the time. Although it is not well known today, it was very popular in the 12th and 13th centuries and was often imitated by other writers, including Master Dogen.[8] Dogen, having spent four years studying Zen in China, was introduced to the *Tso-Ch'an I* during his stay there. Dogen not only imitated the style and tone of the *Tso-Ch'an I*, he borrowed entire sections verbatim and placed them into the *Fukanzazengi*. But Dogen's motivation was, as he himself points out, to correct errors and ambiguities in the *Tso-Ch'an I*, which he felt failed to transmit "the inexpressible heart of the Buddha-patriarchs." Dogen addressed this in his *Fukanzazengi senjutsu yurai* (Reason for Composing *Fukanzazengi*) when he wrote:

> Since in Japan it has never been possible to learn about the "special transmission outside the

---

[8] Gregory, p. 151-2.

scriptures" or the "treasure of the right Dharma eye," much less the principles of zazen, they are not transmitted here [in Japan]. So as soon as I returned home from the land of the Sung [China], and students began coming to me for instruction, I was obliged for their sake to compile this work [Fukanzazengi] on the principles of zazen. Long ago, the Chinese Zen master Po-chang constructed a monastery with a hall set aside especially for zazen practice. In so doing he effectively transmitted the true style of the First Zen patriarch Bodhidharma. This style was distinct from the briars and brambles of word-attachment [of the Buddhist schools] that had preceded him. This is something that students should know and not be confused about.

There is a *Tso-ch'an i* (Japanese, *Zazengi*) by the priest Chang-lu Tsung–tse included in the Ch'an-yüan ch'ing-kuei [Pure Regulations for the Zen Gardens]. For the most part it follows Po-chang's original intent, but it also contains some additions made by Tsung-tse himself. This has resulted in errors of various kinds, as well as an overall lack of clarity. No one who does not already know the meaning behind the words can fully understand what he is trying to say. For that reason, I have now gathered together and written down the true principles of zazen that I learned [in Sung China] in hopes that they will transmit the inexpressible heart of the Buddha-patriarchs.[9]

Although there are some broad similarities as well as identical passages in both works, Dogen's writing is – it could be argued – more beautiful and more poetic. As well, Dogen's work is more profound, inviting the reader to go further in his or her own practice and not to be satisfied with a mere encounter of the absolute. It's also worth noting that the *Tso-Ch'an I* makes almost no reference whatsoever to any koans, whereas Dogen's *Fukanzazengi* makes reference to well over a dozen. Dogen, as we saw earlier, had a thorough training in koan study during his many years at Kenninji temple, so it's only natural that he would make reference to them in his writing – which Dogen did throughout his lifetime.

Today, Master Dogen is revered as an eloquent writer of great passion and insight. His *Kana Shobogenzo* comprises 95 essays and his *Mana Shobogenzo* is a collection of 300 koans with his commentaries. Although Dogen was a prolific writer, his work, however beautiful, inspiring and insightful, remained in almost total obscurity until the early part of the twentieth century. The only people anywhere who had access to Dogen's writing for many centuries were those within the Soto school of Zen. And even within the Soto School, it was mostly literate monks (only about 10% of the members) and Soto scholars who had any access to it or, for that matter, even knew of its

---

[9] Waddell and Abe. *The Heart of Dogen's Shobogenzo*. p. 2.

existence. Some of Dogen's writing was inexplicably lost for hundreds of years until found much later in the treasury of nobles in Kyoto. Dogen's *Bendowa* (*On the Endeavor of the Way*), his second essay composed in 1231, was not found until the late 17th century when it was discovered in a temple in Kyoto – and what is considered to be the original manuscript of *Bendowa* was not found until 1926, some 675 years after Dogen's death.[10]

Furthermore, as incredible as it may seem, a new version of the *Fukanzazengi* was discovered in 1922 when it was suddenly put on display at Tokyo Imperial University. This singular event took Buddhist scholars and academics by surprise since they were completely unaware of any other version of the *Fukanzazenki* except the one in existence at the time. This new text, written on a single scroll, is owned by Eiheiji temple and is extremely well preserved. The paper is thought to be of Sung era (960-1279) manufacture and the script is in the Sung style. Both the writing and Dogen's signature are in accord with known and established writing and signatures of Dogen. The state of preservation is such that scholars believe that it was likely unhandled for many centuries and scholarly research has not found any evidence prior to 1922 that the Soto school was even aware of its existence. This copy of the *Fukanzazengi* is, then, thought to be the earliest known version, dating

---

[10] For more information on how Dogen's works were lost for centuries, see the introduction in Dogen, *The Wholehearted Way*. See also Dogen, "Dogen's 'Bendowa,'" pp. 124-127.

from the first year of the Tenpuku era (1233). The other known copy of the *Fukanzazengi*, which has been in circulation for centuries in the Soto school, is now seen as a revised version that was written a decade or more later.[11] We know, however, that the *Fukanzazengi* was first written in 1227, because at the end of *Bendowa* Dogen states that, "The procedures of meditation should be carried out in accordance with the *Fukan zazen gi*, composed during the Karoku era (1225-27)." The Karoku era ended only a few months after Dogen's return to Japan, so it is therefore probable that he must have written it almost immediately upon his return to Japan from China.

It is only since fairly recently, then, that Master Dogen's work has become known to a wider audience outside the confines of the Soto school. His writing is now available in multiple languages to almost anyone with an interest in reading him. Whether or not there exists other writing by Dogen that has not yet been discovered is anyone's guess.

---

[11] See Bielefeldt, *Dogen's Manuals of Zen Meditation*, p. 15-17. For a comparison of the two versions, see chapter 6.

Fukanzazengi[12]

Eihei Dogen[13]

The Way is basically perfect and all pervading. How could it be contingent upon practice and realization? The Dharma-vehicle is free and untrammeled. What need is there for concentrated effort? Indeed, the whole body is far beyond the world's dust. Who could believe in a means to brush it clean? It is never apart from one, right where one is. What is the use of going off here and there to practice?

---

[12] This translation was originally published in "The Eastern Buddhist," Vol. 6, No. 2, October 1973. pp. 115-128.

[13] Dogen's original manuscript, thought to be in his own hand, is untitled. See Carl Bielefeldt, *Dogen's Manuals of Zen Meditation*, p. 173.

And yet, if there is the slightest discrepancy, the Way is as distant as heaven from earth. If the least like or dislike arises, the Mind is lost in confusion. Suppose one gains pride of understanding and inflates one's own enlightenment, glimpsing the wisdom that runs through all things, attaining the Way and clarifying the Mind, raising an aspiration to escalade the very sky. One is making the initial, partial excursions about the frontiers but is still somewhat deficient in the vital Way of total emancipation.

Need I mention the Buddha, who was possessed of inborn knowledge? The influence of his six years of upright sitting is noticeable still. Or Bodhidharma's transmission of the mind-seal? The fame of his nine years of wall-sitting is celebrated to this day. Since this was the case with the saints of old, how can we today dispense with negotiation of the Way?

You should therefore cease from practice based on intellectual understanding, pursuing words and following after speech, and learn the backward step that turns your light inwardly to illuminate your self. Body and mind of themselves will drop away, and your original face will be manifest. If you want to attain suchness, you should practice suchness without delay.

For sanzen (zazen), a quiet room is suitable. Eat and drink moderately. Cast aside all involvements and cease all affairs. Do not think good or bad. Do not administer pros and cons. Cease all the movements of the conscious mind, the gauging of all thoughts and views. Have no designs on becoming a Buddha. Zazen has nothing whatsoever to do with sitting or lying down.

At the site of your regular sitting, spread out thick matting and place a cushion above it. Sit either in the full-lotus or half-lotus position. In the full-lotus position, you first place your right foot on your left thigh and your left foot on your right thigh. In the half-lotus, you simply press your left foot against your right thigh. You should have your robes and belt loosely bound and arranged in order. Then place your right hand on your left leg and your left palm (facing upwards) on your right palm, thumb-tips touching. Thus sit upright in correct bodily posture, neither inclining to the left nor to the right, neither leaning forward nor backward. Be sure your ears are on a plane with your shoulders and your nose in line with your navel. Place your tongue against the front roof of your mouth, with teeth and lips both shut. Your eyes should always remain open, and you should breathe gently through your nose.

Once you have adjusted your posture, take a deep breath, inhale and exhale, rock your body right and left and settle into a steady, immobile sitting position. Think not-thinking. How do you think not-thinking? Non-thinking. This in itself is the essential art of zazen.

The zazen I speak of is not learning meditation. It is simply the Dharma gate of repose and bliss, the practice-realization of totally culminated enlightenment. It is the manifestation of ultimate reality. Traps and snares can never reach it. Once its heart is grasped, you are like the dragon when he gains the water, like the tiger when she enters the mountain. For you must know that just there (in zazen) the right Dharma is manifesting itself and that, from the first, dullness and distraction are struck aside.

When you arise from sitting, move slowly and quietly, calmly and deliberately. Do not rise suddenly or abruptly. In surveying the past, we find that transcendence of both unenlightenment and enlightenment, and dying while either sitting or standing, have all depended entirely on the strength (of zazen).

In addition, the bringing about of enlightenment by the opportunity provided by a finger, a banner, a needle, or a mallet, and the effecting of realization with the aid of a hossu, a fist, a staff, or a shout, cannot be fully understood by discriminative thinking. Indeed, it cannot be fully known by the practicing or realizing of supernatural powers, either. It must be deportment beyond hearing and seeing – is it not a principle that is prior to knowledge and perceptions?

This being the case, intelligence or lack of it does not matter: between the dull and the sharp-witted there is no distinction. If you concentrate your effort single-mindedly, that in itself is negotiating the Way. Practice realization is naturally undefiled. Going forward (in practice) is a matter of everydayness.

In general, this world, and other worlds as well, both in India and China, equally hold the Buddha-seal, and over all prevails the character of this school, which is simply devotion to sitting, total engagement in immobile sitting. Although it is said that there are as many minds as there are persons, still they all negotiate the way solely in zazen. Why leave behind the seat that exists in your home and go aimlessly off to the dusty realms of other lands? If you make one misstep, you go astray from the Way directly before you.

You have gained the pivotal opportunity of human form. Do not use your time in vain. You are maintaining the essential working of the Buddha-Way. Who would take wasteful delight in the spark from the flintstone? Besides, form and substance are like the dew on the grass, destiny like the dart of lightning – emptied in an instant, vanished in a flash.

Please, honored followers of Zen, long accustomed to groping for the elephant, do not be suspicious of the true dragon. Devote your energies to a way that directly indicates the absolute. Revere the person of complete attainment who is beyond all human agency. Gain accord with the enlightenment of the buddhas; succeed to the legitimate lineage of the ancestors' samadhi. Constantly perform in such a manner and you are assured of being a person such as they. Your treasure-store will open of itself, and you will use it at will.

Fukanzazengi

Commentary

Meeting the True Dragon

The Way is originally perfect and all pervading.

What an amazing first sentence – it's all right there in just eight words. Master Dogen begins the *Fukanzazengi* by telling us that everything, just as it is right now, is perfect – and not only that, but there is nowhere that this perfection does not reach. The "Way" here does not refer to a limited, narrow or personal "way" but rather to the Great Reality of all existence, which is unquantifiable, ungraspable and unlimited. It is boundless. This is the Way that Zen practitioners aspire to realize – in other words, it is the realization of the Great Reality that Master Dogen tells us here is all pervading. Everything is nothing but the Way – and it's perfect. That's it. Everything, seen and unseen, is perfect. This perfection, however, must be realized as that which has no opposite, nor is there any relative scale whereby we can assess its degree of perfection. This perfection is not the perfect of the perfect–imperfect dichotomy to which we are accustomed. This perfection is, quite simply, that which *is*, which is no other than the Great Reality or, as Master Dogen puts it, the Way. It is the completeness of this present moment, lacking nothing. We cannot add anything to this moment nor can we take anything away. This is the complete perfection of *just this*. Elsewhere Master Dogen calls this "genjokoan," or "full manifestation of ultimate reality." What is this genjokoan? Master Dogen says, "It is just all Buddhas in the ten directions and all ancestors, ancient and present, and it is fully manifesting right now. Do you all see it?" Can we see this genjokoan? Can we see this perfect and all-pervading Way? What is it? Dogen says, "It is just our present rolling up the curtain and letting down the curtain, getting up and getting down from the platform. Why don't you all join with me and practice this excellent genjokoan?"[14] It's right here, right now, before our very eyes and in our very ears. It is *all* pervading and there is nowhere that it is not.

How could it be contingent upon practice and realization?

Since the Way is always here – right here, right now – how could its existence be based on whether or not someone is practicing or whether or not someone has had

---

[14] Leighton, p. 117.

realization? How could it be? It's not. So this perfection that Master Dogen is talking about is always right here, right now, wherever we are, whatever we are doing. It is not contingent upon our meditation practice nor is it contingent upon our realizing it. We may not practice meditation, yet the Way is always here. We may not have realization, yet the Way is always here. It does not depend on anything or any activity. It's always right in front of our eyes whether we realize it or not. It is not contingent upon – nor does it depend upon – anything at all. It's like the vast blue sky. It doesn't depend upon our seeing it for it to exist. It may be a cloudy day and the blue sky is obscured from our sight, but it is there nevertheless, whether we see it or not. We may also be looking for the clear blue sky in all the wrong places, such as down a hole or in a thicket. But, nevertheless, the sky is always there whether we see it or not. The Way is not contingent upon anything whatsoever.

The Dharma-vehicle is free and untrammeled.

The Dharma-vehicle here refers to the Way. Dharma, in this case, is simply another word for the Way or the Great Reality and the teachings that surround it. Being free is another way of saying that it pervades everywhere, that everything, everywhere, at this very moment in time and space, is *it*. One way of looking at Dharma-vehicle is to see it as that which brings us to the Dharma or to the Truth. Here we are on a lovely spring afternoon, wondering, perhaps, how do we realize our true nature, how do we experience the absolute? Feeling restricted and blocked in my limited, small self, how do I experience a more fluid, vaster and more spacious self? What is the vehicle for this? When I want to go to the shops in town I wonder to myself, what vehicle will take me there? Perhaps I will take a car, a bicycle or I will walk. For experiencing one's true nature – the oneness of the universe – what vehicle will take me there? Well, just this moment will take me there. How could it be otherwise? This is why it's "free and untrammeled." It's this moment right here and right now – wherever we are that is our entrance to the Way. In fact, it *is* the Way itself! It's unshackled, unlocked, unguarded and open to the public! There are no restrictions. The door is wide open for anyone to pass through. However, the realization of this is another matter, and this may incur many years or many lifetimes of practice. Or not. The sudden realization of oneness may come to anyone in a flash, in an instant and completely out of the blue, anywhere at anytime. We are here in the midst of it and yet we may not yet realize it. It is not separate from ourself.

What need is there for concentrated effort?

Master Dogen poses a rhetorical question, which he has full intention of answering. Since the Way is inherently free from obstruction, since it's all right here in this moment wherever we are, why should anyone make any effort at all? Wouldn't that be pointless? There are people who believe that since the Way is already here and pervades everywhere, there is no need for anyone to make any effort to come to realization. In other words, since we are already intrinsically enlightened, that is to say, since we are already the Way, the Great Reality, living it day in and day out, what's the point of trying to realize something that we already are? Why not just say, "It's my life," or "This is it," and get on with it? If we are fully manifesting ultimate reality by such simple activity as rolling up a curtain or climbing down from a platform, as Dogen says, what need is there, then, for any kind of effort on our part? If zazen, or "just sitting," is "itself the direct realization of the enlightened Buddha mind within us all,"[15] what need is there of direct and immediate realization? Why do we have to do anything?

This is precisely the question that Master Dogen is asking. If we were to stop here and simply claim that our zazen is enlightenment itself, that our life is enlightenment and therefore we need not direct ourselves "towards the absolute" (as Master Dogen urges us to do later on in the *Fukanzazengi*), then Dogen's Zen would be nothing more than dull and lifeless meditation based on the false belief that our deluded way of experiencing the world is in fact the enlightened mind and therefore no determination or effort is necessary. Perhaps interpreting this to be the case, Mujaku Dochu (1653-1745), a well known Japanese Zen practitioner and academic, called Dogen's Zen "pitiable," and D. T. Suzuki, the well known 20th century Rinzai scholar, was

---

[15] Bielefeldt, *Dogen's Manuals of Zen Meditation*, p. 4.

critical of Dogen, calling Dogen's phrase of dropped off body and mind "mere negativism," and Dogen's emphasis on just sitting as "mental stasis." Even Zen Master Hakuin was critical of the Soto school's "silent illumination."[16] But is Master Dogen merely suggesting that we simply accept our delusion as enlightenment and therefore not strive to realize our true nature? Not at all, as we shall soon see.

Indeed, the whole body is far beyond the world's dust.

Master Dogen is making an allusion to the story of the sixth Zen Patriarch, Huineng, who lived in 7th century China. Huineng was an illiterate lumberjack who lived with his mother in southern China. One day while bringing wood to the local village he heard a Buddhist monk reciting the Diamond sutra and he had a spontaneous realization. Huineng asked the monk where he had learned such a thing and the monk told him that he studied with the Fifth Patriarch up in the north. Huineng decided to go and visit the monastery where the Fifth Patriarch lived and taught. Huineng travelled to the Fifth Patriarch's monastery and asked him if he could live and study there. The Fifth Patriarch asked him where he had come from and Huineng responded that he had come from the south. The Fifth Patriarch commented that

---

[16] Bielefeldt, *Dogen's Manuals of Zen Meditation*. p. 4. Access to Dogen's writing for Hakuin would have been limited as he was not in the Soto School. However, commentaries on the Shobogenzo began to be published in the 18th century and Hakuin would have probably had access to those.

Buddha nature didn't exist in the south, which was a little poke of a stick to test Huineng. Huineng said, "Although there are northern men and southern men, north and south make no difference to their Buddha nature." Hearing this, the Fifth Patriarch said he could stay and put him to work in the kitchen.

At some point during Huineng's time at the monastery, the Fifth Patriarch decided to have a contest to see which of his monks could write the best poem. The winner, he said, would become his successor. The head monk wrote the following poem and put it on the wall for all to see:

> The body is the wisdom-tree,
> The mind is a bright mirror stand,
> Take care to wipe it all the time,
> And allow no dust to cling.

Although this is a poem that demonstrates a certain understanding, it lacks the insight of a thoroughgoing breakthrough, a clear realization of one's true nature. Realization may be shallow or deep, and this poem, lovely as it is, reflects a somewhat shallow understanding, lacking a truly clear comprehension of the Great Reality.

The Sixth Patriarch saw the poem on the wall but, being illiterate, had to ask a monk to read him the poem, which the monk did. The Sixth Patriarch then asked the monk if he would write down his own poem if he dictated it to him. The monk agreed, wrote it down, and Huineng hung it on the wall next to the first poem.

> Fundamentally no wisdom-tree exists,
> Nor the stand of a mirror bright,
> Since all is empty from the beginning,
> Where can the dust alight?

This poem demonstrates a deep enlightenment, a clear realization, and this was certainly not lost on the Fifth Patriarch who, when he read it, knew immediately who had written it.

Now we come back to Master Dogen's sentence about the whole body being beyond the world's dust, which refers to the poems of the head monk and the Sixth Patriarch. It's almost as if Dogen is inviting us to see that we ourselves are beyond our own dust, since from the beginning everything is perfect, just as it is. In other words, everything is empty. There is no wisdom-tree, no mirror stand, not even any dust.

Who could believe in a means to brush it clean?

There is no brush, no mirror, no stand and no dust. There is nothing to alight and nowhere for this nothing to land. This emptiness pervades everywhere, but even "pervades" is too much since from the beginningless beginning there is nothing anywhere. If we truly see nothing, then, as Master Dogen himself puts it, we are enlightened by everything.[17] Seeing our own emptiness, we see the emptiness of all phenomena and are at once enlightened by them – in fact, at this moment, all phenomena are enlightened as there is nothing *but* enlightenment. Our own enlightenment is therefore the enlightenment of the entire universe, unimaginably boundless and limitless. When we awaken, everyone and everything awakens. What is there to brush clean?

It is never apart from one, right where one is.

Master Dogen brings us back to *this*, right here, right now. This is it, whatever this is. Take a look around you. Listen to the sounds. Inhale the scents of your room. Feel your body. Be aware of your thoughts. This is it, right here. The Great Reality is never separate from you, ever. You *are* it. It is not somewhere else. It is not far away and it is not near.

As we chant in "The Identity of Relative and Absolute:"[18]

> If you do not see the Way, you do not see it even as you walk on it. When you walk the Way, it is not near, it is not far. If you are deluded, you are mountains and rivers away from it.

---

[17] See Master Dogen's *Genjokoan*: "To forget the self is to be enlightened by the ten thousand dharmas (all phenomena)."
[18] An 8th century Chinese poem written by Sekito Kisen and chanted during Zen ceremonies.

We are all, right now, at this very moment, manifesting the Great Reality, beaming it through our entire body. We *are* it. This is the perfection that is beyond perfect and imperfect. Now we must truly realize this!

What's the use of going off here and there to practice?

Since it's all right here where we stand at this very moment, why should we make any effort to practice? Why should we do anything? It's all right here! That's what Master Dogen is saying, almost agreeing with those who might think that there is no need to strive for enlightenment or make any concerted effort. Of course, Dogen himself not only went off "here and there" to practice Zen, he left his own country to study Zen in China. This was in 13th century Japan when travel was much more difficult than it is today. But as we shall see, Dogen is setting the stage for an unfolding drama of why, in effect, we must make an effort to practice and come to our own realization of the Way. Once we continue reading a bit further we'll see that we've been set up, and Dogen is ready to unleash the full force of his deep realization through his linguistic prowess.

And yet, if there is the slightest discrepancy, the Way is as distant as heaven from earth.

And now Master Dogen begins to sow seeds of doubt in what he has just told us. Everything seemed free and easy with all things being perfect and the Way being right here and right now at this very moment. How simple it seemed to manifest ultimate reality! But Dogen suddenly throws us down a hole with this apparently innocuous beginning, *"And yet,"* followed by the heretofore unforeseen possibility of what he calls a "slight discrepancy," as if we were accountants trying to get expenditure figures to match in a ledger. How could the Way be far apart from us, as distant as heaven and earth, if it's right here, right now? What could we be missing and what is this "slight discrepancy" that Master Dogen is talking about? How could the Way be distant from anything if we *are* the Way?

If the least like or dislike arises, the Mind is lost in confusion.

The *Mind* referred to here is the Way and not our discursive, analytical or rational mind with which we think and solve problems or puzzles. This is the all-encompassing Big Mind and not our narrow, limited small mind. This Mind is boundless, limitless and formless. It is the Way. It is always here and yet (and yet!) we can lose this Mind in a sea of confusion. Not that it goes anywhere or disappears, it's just that we no longer recognize it or realize it. Dogen tells us that Mind is lost when the slightest "like or dislike arises" in our thoughts. This is the activity of our small mind which is full of its own opinions, ideas, concepts and points of view. It likes this but not that. It wants this one but not that one. It believes this idea is good but this other idea is bad. This very activity of picking and choosing aids in the solidification of the small mind, in cementing its place apart from other small minds and other phenomena. This creates its individuality, its distinctiveness and it works tirelessly to maintain this sense of separation. The small mind wants to run the show, to make us believe that it is so important, and in doing so the Mind is, quite simply, lost in confusion. We believe that our ideas and our concepts – which are simply constructs of our small mind – are somehow the truth. In other words, our thoughts become solidified by virtue of our beliefs, and our core belief is that whatever we think or whatever we conceive of is the truth. Or the opposite. We may also identify as being wrong, so whatever we think of is wrong and we are perpetually at fault. Either way, it comes back to the solidification of what we believe or what we think. This is being lost in confusion.

Suppose one gains pride of understanding and inflates one's own enlightenment, glimpsing the wisdom that runs through all things, attaining the Way and clarifying the Mind, raising an aspiration to escalade the very sky.

Can we truly appreciate what it's like to feel proud of our understanding, of our own enlightenment? What kind of pride is this? Can we see that? When we glimpse the absolute, that is to say, when we have a shallow experience of enlightenment, we don't yet know that it's merely a glimpse or a partial experience of the Great Reality. We may believe that it's a clear breakthrough. For many of us, and especially if it's our first awakening, we have nothing else with which we are able to compare it. We may even feel superior to others who don't yet see what we see. This is the pride that Master Dogen is talking about. *Look what I can see!* And yet, as ridiculous as it may seem, this is perhaps not an uncommon occurrence since even Zen Master Hakuin wrote about it soon after his great enlightenment: "My pride soared up like a majestic mountain, my arrogance surged forward like the tide."[19] Other contemporary Zen masters have written about it as well. Koryu Osaka Roshi, one of Maezumi Roshi's teachers, had the following to say about arrogance in our practice:

> When you start studying koans, and pass a few of them, you may feel that you understand Zen. You may even become arrogant and conceited. Self-satisfaction, whether it occurs in the beginning stages of koan practice or after you have completed koan study, impedes further progress.[20]

Genpo Roshi, the second Dharma heir of Maezumi Roshi, stated that after having had an awakening experience in the desert he attended a retreat at the Zen Center of Los Angeles in 1972. At one point during the retreat Maezumi Roshi said to him, "You are the most arrogant young man I have ever met."[21]

---

[19] Yampolsky, p. 118.
[20] Maezumi, p. 80. Koryu Osaka Roshi (1901 – 1985) was a lay Rinzai teacher and Dharma heir of Hannyakutsu Joko Roshi.
[21] Merzel, p. 59. See also p. 58 where Genpo Roshi talks about his inflated ego regarding his enlightenment experience.

After having struggled so hard to achieve some kind of breakthrough, why wouldn't we feel pride at our accomplishment? The pride of enlightenment occurs because we are finally "glimpsing the wisdom that runs through all things," while simultaneously adding something else on top of it: our own self-satisfaction of attainment – even at the expense of others! How ridiculous! And we want our attainment to become clearer and clearer and clearer. It almost becomes an obsession. This clarity that we have, however partial or limited, becomes the focus of our attention and we may eventually do everything we can to make it brighter and brighter, clearer and clearer, as if we were diligently polishing the dust from a mirror. We may even want our clarity to be so clear that it blinds everyone else, like driving around in our car at night with the high beams on. We are so attached to this clarity that we feel as if we could climb to the highest heights of the sky! And don't let anyone get in our way! It's absolutely and completely absurd, but that's the "aspiration to escalade the very sky." What we do not realize at this stage is that this sort of clarity and being so intensely focused on the absolute serves no one except perhaps our own ego. It's not until we choose to be in the muddy waters with everyone else that we may perhaps begin to help others and do some good.

One is making the initial, partial excursions about the frontiers but it is still somewhat deficient in the vital Way of total emancipation.

Exploring the frontiers of one's own realization is part of the maturation process of enlightenment. These frontiers are not fixed demarcation lines but rather how we manifest our realization in our lives – how is our newfound perspective allowing us to appreciate situations in different ways and how are our ingrained habits still continuing to operate without our being aware of them. These are the initial stages of actualizing our realization. As Master Dogen writes, we are still not fully emancipated. We are just beginning our exploration of this new perspective, which is none other than approaching the world from the absolute reality rather than the relative reality we have known so well. It's the same world, of course, but our point of view is inconceivably different. In many ways we are like little children exploring our new environment, but we are not quite there yet. Actualizing the "vital Way of total emancipation" may take many, many years of training and it will not be fully embodied until we have transcended our own enlightenment and have seen through it completely. This is of crucial importance because otherwise we solidify our enlightenment experience and make something solid out of it without ever seeing that the absolute is, in fact, empty.

Need I mention the Buddha, who was possessed of inborn knowledge? The influence of his six years of upright sitting is noticeable still.

Buddha means "awakened one," and is commonly used to refer to Siddhartha Gautama who had a deep realization and then taught for forty years sometime in 600 BC or so. Master Dogen recognizes here that the Buddha possessed an innate wisdom, intelligence and perspicacity that was perhaps rare among his peers. But was that enough? Was this knowledge enough to liberate him from suffering? In other words, could he figure out how to be content and liberated with his discursive mind? Dogen's subtle response is a resounding no. No matter how intelligent or wise one is, one is still unable to realize one's true nature through the discursive mind. It is not Buddha's inborn knowledge that influences us to this very day – it's his six years of upright sitting. The Buddha meditated diligently for six years, enduring innumerable hardships and suffering in an effort to liberate himself. This was not an intellectual process of liberation, it was, rather, a lot of work. Siddhartha finally experienced a breakthrough, a deep realization of the oneness of life. The effort of those six years reverberates and resonates to this very day – to this very moment! That's what Dogen is saying, that all the effort of Siddhartha Gautama from 2,600 years ago is still noticeable today.

Or Bodhidharma's transmission of the mind-seal? The fame of his nine years of wall sitting is celebrated to this day.

Now Master Dogen invokes Bodhidharma, the Indian monk who brought the Buddha's teachings from India to China in the sixth century. Bodhidharma is often affectionately referred to as the Western Barbarian because he came from the West (from India to China) and also because he was reputed to be very large and unkempt. But initially he left China by crossing the Yangtze River and then traveled to Shaolin Monastery on Mount Song. At the monastery he took up residence in the East Hall and did nothing but zazen all day long. The other monks couldn't figure him out, calling him the wall-gazing Brahmin. For nine years he did zazen and didn't speak of the Dharma. He became famous for his zazen and wall facing. He also wrote this well-known four-line stanza:

> A special transmission outside the scriptures,
> Not depending on words and letters;
> Directly pointing to the mind
> Seeing into one's true nature and attaining Buddhahood.

This "special transmission outside the scriptures," which is not dependent upon words, letters, books or any kind of writing, is the mind-seal of Bodhidharma and has been passed on from generation to generation. Master Dogen again emphasizes the zazen of an ancient patriarch,

Bodhidharma, which is still influencing us to this very day, and not only the zazen of this old master, but the many years of hard practice that he endured. How many of us would sit facing a wall for nine years?

Since this was the case with the saints of old, how can we today dispense with negotiation of the Way?

And now, having set the stage, Master Dogen reveals his true intentions. If the sages of the past had to work so hard to attain the Way, to realize their true nature and spend years actualizing their realization day after day, why should anyone today who wants to realize the Great Reality be given a pass? Since it's all right here, at this very moment, what's the use of making an effort to practice? Having an idea or a concept that everything is *it*, that the Way is right here, right now, wherever we are, is, quite simply, not enough. We must have realization in order to truly see the Way, to manifest the Way and actualize our understanding day in and day out. As Dogen is alluding to here, attaining the Way and manifesting our realization in our daily lives is hard work. An enlightenment experience may come out of nowhere – suddenly, unbidden like a ripe blackberry falling from its stem to our tongues – but actualizing this experience, moment after moment, is the practice of a lifetime – endlessly profound, boundless and infinite. It goes on forever. This is what Master Hakuin's teacher Shoju Roshi called, "Continuous and unremitting devotion to hidden practice, scrupulous application –

that is the essence within the essence."[22] So if this was the case for the ancient Zen masters, how is it that we could dispense with our own arduous negotiation of the Way?

You should therefore cease from practice based on intellectual understanding, pursuing words and following after speech, and learn the backward step that turns your light inwardly to illuminate your self.

Master Dogen is coming at us with direct instructions on how to negotiate the Way. Practice based on intellectual understanding is, to a large extent, inevitable at the beginning of our spiritual quest. Even if we have had some kind of glimpse of the absolute, of our true nature, we often approach practice based on what we have heard or what we have read. In fact, we sometimes even privilege reading about practice more than the actual practice itself. We cling to words and build large and complex constructions out of ideas and concepts. We read books, sutras or koans and exclaim, *Ah ha! This is it!* And in doing so we solidify something – an idea, a concept, a point of view, whatever it may be. We cling to it like a life preserver in a rough sea, holding on for dear life. Our meditation practice becomes based on an idea that we have in our mind. Our understanding of Zen, of the Way, is thus a mental construct built from our opinions and concepts. Dogen is telling us to stop chasing after language, stop trying to figure out what the Way is. The fundamental point here is that the Way will

---

[22] Waddell, *Wild Ivy*, p. 35.

not be found outside of ourselves in something that we read, hear or even think about. This is, "pursuing words and following after speech." Our minds are adept at thinking, and this thinking, which is useful for solving pragmatic problems and achieving certain goals, is not helpful in realizing our true nature.

Instead of looking for the Truth outside of ourselves, Master Dogen tells us to turn our light inwards and illuminate ourselves. This phrase is borrowed from Zen Master Rinzai who lived and taught some 400 years before Dogen. Master Rinzai said, when speaking to his assembly, "Turn your own light inward upon yourselves."[23] Our own liberation will not be found in the daily chants, in the sutras, in the many books on Zen or in talks given by teachers. This is not to say that we cannot benefit and be inspired by these various means of teaching, but they are not the Great Reality, just as a map is not the terrain and a picture of a flag does not wave in the wind. These may point to the Truth, but they are not the Truth itself. These words and phrases are merely sign posts indicating the Way, such as we often come across when driving in a car. Who among us, when seeing a sign for New York City, would pull over and get out and exclaim, *We're here!* In the same way, words and phrases are not *it*, and yet they are not apart from *it*, but we must keep going until we realize the Way ourselves. The only place that we will find awakening is in our own life, right

---

[23] Rinzai, p. 28.

now, at this very moment. It's all right here. How could it be otherwise?

Body and mind of themselves will drop away, and your original face will be manifest.

The dropping away of body and mind is the experience of enlightenment, of realizing our true nature, the oneness of all phenomena. However, the word "experience" is inherently lacking here since, in a strict sense, when there is dropping away of body and mind, there is no one to experience anything. There is nothing and there is no one there to experience this realization, there is simply the realization that is being realized. This is the vast emptiness of Bodhidharma.[24] It is the realization of what is right here, right now without any filter of "me." There is no temporal or spatial aspect – in other words, it is timeless and without separation and therefore without distance. Space and time are seen through as non-existent. This is our "original face" to which Dogen is referring, citing here a famous phrase: "Show me your face before your parents were born."[25] To realize this we must turn our light inward and illuminate our self – as Master Rinzai urges us to do – instead of seeking outside of ourselves which is what we normally do. Dropping away of body and mind is the Great Liberation of all the past Buddhas, sages and Zen masters

---

[24] When Emperor Wu of Liang asked Bodidharma, "What is the first principle of the holy teaching?" Bodhidharma replied, "Vast emptiness, nothing holy."
[25] The words of the Sixth Patriarch to the pursuing Monk Myo.

– it is the birthright of each one of us. We may begin with only a slight dropping away of body and mind which is a glimpse of the absolute, a shallow experience of our true nature and our original face, but in time this dropping away of body and mind may occur to the greater degree to which Dogen is referring and then everything will be clear.

If you want to attain suchness, you should practice suchness without delay.

Attaining suchness is the realization of our true nature, dropping off body and mind – this is enlightenment. This is the liberation of Siddhartha Gautama and the great patriarchs of the past. It is the liberation of the great Zen teachers of today. This is the liberation of each one of us. This suchness is the vast emptiness of Bodhidharma, and Dogen here tells us that if we want to attain this realization we must practice this realization "without delay." In our lineage of Zen the timekeeper reminds us at the end of the day of the importance of not wasting our time:

> Let me respectfully remind you, life and death are of supreme importance, time swiftly passes by and opportunity is lost, let us awaken. Awaken! Take heed, do not squander your life.

Not squandering one's life is "without delay." Days pass quickly, weeks fly by and the years speed past like galloping horses. When are we going to devote ourselves – our lives – to realizing the Way and actualizing it in our everyday activity? Part of our ceremonial service is the recitation of "The Identity of Relative and Absolute," a 32-line poem written by Sekito Kisen in eighth century China, which ends with the following two lines: "I respectfully say to those who wish to be enlightened: Do not waste your time by night or day." Again, we are reminded of the importance of not wasting or squandering our time and Master Dogen instructs us to practice suchness if we want to realize our true nature. But what does that mean to practice suchness? Practicing suchness is no other than zazen, and when we practice zazen we manifest our true nature with the faith that one day we will have realization and exclaim, as Yasutani Roshi mentioned, *Ah ha! This is it!*[26] Master Dogen will now kindly give us detailed instruction on how to practice suchness.

For zazen, a quiet room is suitable. Eat and drink moderately.

In the beginning, a quiet room will do. This atmosphere will help us focus and allow us to concentrate on our meditation. As we continue our practice through the years we'll inevitably come to find that we can do zazen anywhere, anytime. We can do it at 35,000 feet in an airplane. We can do it in a car, on a beach or on a crowded train. Zazen can be done anywhere and it makes little or no difference whether the room is quiet or

---

[26] See page 54, footnote 29.

not. Eventually, over time, we may even come to see that all of our activity throughout the day is nothing but zazen: walking to the store, talking to a friend, riding a bicycle, brushing our teeth. This ordinary, everyday activity – it's all zazen.

Not eating or drinking to excess will also help us on the cushion in the sense that we have not overindulged in food or drink. If we do, our attention may be unnecessarily drawn to the efforts that our stomach and digestive track must make. It is better to eat and drink in moderation.

Cast aside all involvements and cease all affairs.

Some of us have the luxury of being able to do just this. Others among us have jobs, families and other obligations that cannot be cast aside, nor would we want to cast them aside. But in Master Dogen's day, most practitioners of Zen were ordained monks living and practicing in a monastery, in a temple or in a remote hermitage. Today, especially in the West, this is rarely the case. However, when we come to sit on the cushion and cross our legs we can, in fact, cast aside absolutely everything and cease all activity. We can really feel as if we were in a small boat pushing off from shore and going way out. Sometimes we come together for a day or a week to meditate intensively, supporting each other in our practice, and these retreats are a precious opportunity to cease all affairs. But what if we were to take Master Dogen's words one step further? What if we were to cast off all of our involvements and cease all of our affairs in the very midst of being involved and conducting transactions? What if there was no one doing anything? What if there were just the doing without someone conducting the action? What if "we" were not there while we were in fact doing something?

Do not think good or bad. Do not administer pros and cons.

This is in reference to the story of the Sixth Patriarch, Huineng. After the Fifth Patriarch read his poem, he invited Huineng back to his quarters at midnight and it was there that he transmitted to him his robe and bowl, signifying the transmission of the Dharma, making Huineng the Sixth Patriarch. Knowing that the other monks would be furious, the Fifth Patriarch instructed Huineng to leave immediately and go into hiding. When the monks learned what had happened, the head monk, Myo – who had written the first poem – became furious and vowed to catch Huineng. He set off at a halting pace and after many hours of running he finally saw him on a trail out in the forest. Seeing the head monk running after him, Huineng stopped and waited. When the head monk caught up to Huineng he demanded the robe and the bowl and Huineng obligingly set them down on the ground and said, "The robe represents our faith. If it's the robe you want, please take it." Myo reached for the robe and the bowl but they were as immovable as a mountain and he was unable to pick them up. Overcome with emotion he cried, "It's not the robe and the bowl that I want, it's the Dharma. Please teach me." And now the Sixth Patriarch, seeing the love and the sincerity in Myo's whole being said, "Think neither good nor evil. At this very moment, what is the True self of monk Myo?" At these words, monk Myo had realization.

Our true self is beyond any concepts or ideas of good or bad. Our mind is constantly evaluating and judging situations, events, thoughts and people. The critical process of our mind is seemingly endless. It is constantly in motion and we become caught up in it believing it to be reality. This is "good" and this is "bad." It's all in our mind. Things *are* just as they *are* without any labels or judgments that we may assign them. This critical thinking is the realm of our discursive mind and is, in effect, its natural function, just as seeing colors is the natural function of the eye and hearing sounds is the natural function of the ears. But what we see, what we hear and what we think are but a few grains of sand on an endless beach that circumnavigates the great earth. There is so much more. Monk Myo was caught up in what he thought was good and bad, but thanks to the compassion of the Sixth Patriarch he was able to come to realization and awaken to his true self.

Cease all the movements of the conscious mind, the gauging of all thoughts and views.

The movements of the conscious mind are our thinking, examining, processing and analyzing – the exegetical apparatus that assigns labels to things, opinions about texts and viewpoints on the state of the world and its affairs. This is our discursive mind, our rational, thinking mind. Dogen tells us to stop following after these thoughts and stop evaluating everything. Master Rinzai said, "Bring to rest the thoughts of the ceaselessly seeking mind, and you will not differ from the patriarch-buddha." The patriarch-buddha is none other than each one of us, but because we are running around seeking the Truth here and there, high and low, near and far, we don't see that it is right here, right now, before our very eyes. Master Rinzai goes on to say that, "The six-rayed divine light never ceases to shine."[27] These six rays of divine light are our seeing, hearing, touching smelling, tasting and thinking. The Way is right before us all day long and into the night. Wherever we go, there it is. To realize this is to be the Buddha. To understand this intellectually, to have an idea or a concept of it in our mind is to be, as Rinzai says, "born in the wombs of asses or cows." This is the gauging of thoughts and views which is the intellectual and conceptual banter of the mind, nothing more than mental constructs which cannot grasp that which is ungraspable.

---

[27] Rinzai, p. 8.

Have no designs on becoming a Buddha.

We can never become a Buddha. It's simply impossible, and the sooner we realize this the sooner we will be a Buddha. There is nothing to become, nothing to attain and nothing to do. In fact, there is simply *nothing*, period. Having designs on becoming a Buddha is an intellectual approach to awakening to our true nature, and no matter how long we search for it, we'll never find it, even if we take comfort in ideas, concepts, words and phrases. We might as well write our attainment down on a magnet and stick it on our refrigerator to read every morning as we make breakfast. The fact is, we are already Buddha. Because we are already manifesting our true nature every moment of the day, we are already the Buddha that we seek. Everyone and everything is Buddha. There is nothing outside of Buddha. But because of our delusion we don't realize it. It would be as if we had designs on becoming a human being. Doesn't that sound ridiculous? We already *are* human beings and could not become one in a million years. This is seeking something outside of ourselves. We must strive to realize our true nature and all of this will become clear.

Zazen has nothing whatsoever to do with sitting or lying down.

The Japanese word "zazen" is composed of two characters: "za" meaning "seated" and "zen" meaning "meditation," so zazen, strictly speaking, means "seated meditation." Master Dogen is telling us that zazen has nothing to do with being seated. Sitting down, lying down, walking, riding a bicycle – this is all zazen. This is a far-reaching perspective of meditation where there is no specific activity that designates a meditative state or posture. There is no special activity that we do that has some special outcome. Our entire life is zazen. Standing in line at the post office is zazen. Signing our name on a traffic ticket is zazen. Sending an email or walking on the beach is also zazen. Zazen is far beyond any defining activity that we may assign to it. It is boundless and infinite. There is nowhere that zazen is not – our entire being is zazen. This is the point that Master Dogen is making here. And now, having clearly stated that zazen has nothing whatsoever to do with sitting, Master Dogen will give us detailed instructions on how to do zazen in the seated posture.

At the site of your regular sitting, spread out thick matting and place a cushion above it.

Isn't that thoughtful of Dogen? He advises us to spread out "thick matting" and put a cushion on top of it. He doesn't say that we should sit on a block of wood or a stone on a hardwood floor. No, he wants us to be comfortable, to settle in for awhile and get into it. There is no need to punish ourselves with a cold environment or a hard floor. A nice, thick mat will do and a cushion on top of it. This is not about asceticism whereby we deprive ourselves of relative comforts needed to sustain long or even short periods of sitting.

Sit either in the full-lotus or half-lotus position. In the full-lotus position, you first place your right foot on your left thigh and your left foot on your right thigh. In the half-lotus, you simply press your left foot against your right thigh. You should have your robes and belt loosely bound and arranged in order. Then place your right hand on your left leg and your left palm (facing upwards) on your right palm, thumb-tips touching. Thus sit upright in correct bodily posture, neither inclining to the left nor to the right, neither leaning forward nor backward. Be sure your ears are on a plane with your shoulders and your nose in line with your navel. Place your tongue against the front roof of your mouth, with teeth and lips both shut. Your eyes should always remain open, and you should breathe gently through your nose.

These concrete instructions are those that we still follow to this day. Note the care with which Dogen instructs us about our posture, aligning the body with relation to the ears, the shoulders, our nose and our navel. We can see that this is no ordinary sitting such as we often do when we are relaxing. For many of us, sitting in half- or full-lotus is all but impossible. Simply sitting cross-legged on a cushion is fine, or with our knees tucked under us in the *seiza* position. Sitting on a chair is also perfectly acceptable and very effective.

Once you have adjusted your posture, take a deep breath, inhale and exhale, rock your body right and left and settle into a steady, immobile sitting position. Think not-thinking. How do you think not-thinking? Non-thinking. This in itself is the essential art of zazen.

After providing us with precise instructions on our physical posture when seated on the cushion, Master Dogen now begins to bring us into the heart of zazen: *Think not-thinking.* Now, how do we do that? Dogen even poses this very question right in the text so that he may respond: *Non-thinking.* Now we are entering the inexpressible heart of the matter: the functioning of our mind and how this relates to our meditation practice. It's an understatement to say that our mind does many things. It's a mystery that science will never completely fathom. For our purposes and with regards to the *Fukanzazengi*, we will look at our mind from the perspective of its thought production.

Thoughts appear in our mind all the time. Their production is a natural function of the brain and may be seen as no more of a hindrance to us than the production of bile from the gallbladder or the production of urine from the kidneys. We may also say, in a very broad sense, that our brain produces thoughts just as our eyes produce sight, our ears produce sound, our nose produces scent, our tongue produces taste and our flesh produces the sensation of touch. Now, there are some who would say that to stop all thought is the main purpose of our meditation. They might argue that we are looking for – to quote a cliché – the "still point" whereby there are no thoughts and our mind is a vast empty space. But trying to suppress thoughts or stop their production is like trying to remove colors from our eyes or sounds from our ears. It would be like trying to erase the color blue from the sky. However, through simple, basic techniques such as counting or following our breath we are able to bring our mind to focus on a task and thus keep it reigned in. These techniques increase our power of concentration while decreasing the chances of the mind wandering off – which is exactly what the mind wants to do. It wants to stay busy and create stories or drama while preparing for the future or ruminating on the past. Simple thoughts lead to sentences which lead to stories and so on and so forth. It's endless! And we believe it's real. But it's all just in our heads, and while we're busy amusing ourselves with our stories, a big black bear wanders by the window! If anything will bring someone right back to the here and now, it's a black bear walking by the window.[28]

Cultivating our power of concentration in zazen is crucial to non-thinking. The power of being able to focus the mind on a task allows for a greater, more spacious awareness to reveal itself during our meditation. This spacious awareness has been there all along, but because we have been so busy thinking, processing and figuring

---

[28] In May 2018 a bear walked by the window at Yokoji Zen Mountain Center in California while we were doing zazen.

things out, it has been largely obscured, much in the same way that clouds obscure the vast sky. Thoughts, as a natural product of the brain, will always occur, but that doesn't mean that we have to pay much attention to them. These thoughts will naturally, and of their own accord, disappear if we don't feed them our undivided attention – and we soon realize that they need our attention in order to exist. Over time, as we pay less and less attention to our thoughts, and especially less attention to the cultivation of thinking, we may find that thought production is vastly reduced, giving way to a more fluid feeling of spaciousness and of non-solidity. In this vast space we may begin to pay more attention to other things (or perhaps nothing at all), such as the sounds around us: the rustle of the leaves outside or the sound of a passing airplane. A cough. The creak of floorboards. There is so much happening in the world of sound. Listen! Within this vast space there are sounds, there is light, there are scents, and there are thoughts. This is non-thinking. This is what Dogen means by the essential art of zazen.

The zazen I speak of is not learning meditation.

Many of us have spent a lot of time in school. Many of us have gone on to university spending years studying various subjects, learning how to write essays and take exams. By the time we reach our early twenties we've been in school almost all of our life. In many ways we are so good at learning, so accustomed to it and so at ease with it that it has almost become second nature to learn something when we do an activity. What would be the point of doing an activity where we didn't learn something? I knew someone who frequently said, "Everyday I want to learn something new." This is an admirable trait, certainly, and in many respects it's indicative of our society as a whole. We always seem to want to get something out of whatever we're doing, whether it be yoga, sports, work, or even our leisure time. We want to learn, even if it's just learning how to do something with less effort or in less time.

The meditation that Master Dogen is talking about is not concerned with learning anything. This is not a class where we take notes. We're not learning new postures. The zazen that Dogen is talking about is not concerned with mulling over our problems and trying to figure out solutions, or sifting through past traumas and trying to come to terms with them. Neither are we processing anything. Processing, learning, figuring out, coming to terms with things – these are all the activity of the discursive mind. Important as these functions are for our daily existence, zazen has no concern for them whatsoever. And although things may come up while we're sitting and we may look at them and be aware of them as they arise and unfold from the depths of our unconscious, we are not actively trying to figure anything out. Nor are we learning anything. We learn nothing in meditation. Zazen, from the standpoint of the discursive mind, is totally and utterly pointless.

It is simply the Dharma gate of repose and bliss, the practice-realization of totally culminated enlightenment.

As we saw earlier, Dharma refers to the Way or the Great Reality and the teachings that surround it. Gate, of course, refers to the entrance to this, the way in, so to speak. Dogen is emphasizing that zazen is a pathway to realization and yet, in the second half of the sentence, he emphasizes the fact that zazen is itself realization in "practice-realization" apart from anything else to obtain or realize.

When we are sitting zazen there is, as mentioned earlier, a spaciousness that may reveal itself during our meditation. The more we practice concentration techniques of focusing the mind – on counting from one to ten, on following our breath or on other sensory observations – the more easily we let go of solidifying our thinking. Thoughts continue to appear, however, but our habitual tendency of following those thoughts and creating stories may eventually diminish as we practice diligently. This is non-thinking. Soon, a whole new space may open up between those thoughts – so to speak – a space that may at first seem unfamiliar and yet, deep down, we may feel as if we are coming home. Although one might think that the thoughts and the space in between the thoughts are different, they are not. They are one seamless flow of consciousness, a wave of awareness that sometimes manifests as thought and sometimes as non-thought. And sometimes it manifests as thinking.

This is beyond thinking and non-thinking, this seamless awareness pervading everywhere. This practice of non-thinking allows for a vast field to reveal itself where the entire universe can show up unimpeded by our thinking: a fly buzzing around our head; dappled sunlight across the floor; the sound of leaves rustling outside the window; the feeling of the cushion under our legs. And then, suddenly, a thought passes. How marvelous! The brain is at work, doing its thing, and then, just as quickly as that thought enters our mind, it vanishes. A door opens in the distance and the sound of footsteps and creaking floorboards fills the air. What else is there? This practice *is* realization, which is Bodhi, or awakening, where all phenomena *are* just as they *are*. This zazen is called *shikantaza*.

Yasutani Roshi[29] said that this practice, *shikantaza*, is "the highest practice," where "means and end coalesce." He went on to say that, "when rightly practiced, you sit in the firm conviction that zazen is the actualization of your undefiled True-nature, *and at the same time you sit in complete faith that the day will come when, exclaiming, "Oh this is it!" you will unmistakably realize this True-nature.*"[30] This is precisely what Master Dogen is referring to when he writes, "the practice-realization of totally culminated enlightenment." Far from being simply a means to an end, zazen is the actualization of our true nature and not

---

[29] Hakuun Yasutani Roshi (1885-1973) was a Dharma heir of Harada Sogaku Roshi (1871-1961) and a teacher of Maezumi Roshi.
[30] Kapleau, p. 46.

simply a technique for achieving enlightenment. However, it is important to experience enlightenment – even to a shallow degree – in order to grasp the truth of this, otherwise we are nothing more than elephant gropers,[31] complacent in our discursive understanding and unconcerned with making Shayamuni's experience our own. On this subject, Zen Master Hakuin considered enlightenment so crucial to one's understanding of Zen that he went so far as to say that anyone who called themselves a follower of Zen and had not realized their true nature was, quite simply, an outright fraud.[32] Yamada Roshi[33] said that attaining enlightenment was "the most important matter," and that without this experience, "there is practically no Zen Buddhism."[34]

It is the manifestation of ultimate reality.

In this meditation, which I mentioned earlier is called *shikantaza*, or *just sitting*, we are not labeling thoughts, sights, sounds, feelings or emotions. We are not adding anything to that which is already there, whatever it may be. In a certain sense, we could say that we are just observing this universe of free-flowing colors, sounds and puffs of ideas, all of which are transmigrating in and out of our sphere of consciousness. We are, quite simply, going along with what *is*, whether it's the sound of the

---

[31] The blind people who all describe an elephant differently as cited by Dogen in the *Fukanzazengi*.
[32] Waddell, *Wild Ivy*, p. 1.
[33] Koun Yamada Roshi (1907-1989) was a Dharma heir of Yasutani Roshi.
[34] Yamada, p. 7-9.

wind, a cool breeze on our neck or a thought popping up in our mind about what we'd like to have for lunch. In this moment, who is it that is observing what? Who is it sitting on a cushion, hearing the sounds, seeing the colors of light and darkness on the floor? Who is hearing the wind outside the window? Who is it? And what if there were just the observing? What if there was no perceivable observer? What if it were just the seeing, the hearing, the smelling, the feeling and the tasting? What if all of these things were going on and yet nobody was home? In other words, if we look at what I just wrote about "going along with what is" and take it even further, as Master Dogen is inviting us to do, what if we were to say that instead of going along with what is, what if *we were what is*, whatever *it is* happens to be? What if, instead of saying that we are just observing this universe, we were to experience that we *were* just this universe? Not observing something on the outside, but *being* all things without the illusion of an inside or an outside. The sound of footsteps. A cool breeze across our neck. A sneeze. As the great Irish poet W. B. Yeats once wrote, "How can we know the dancer from the dance?"[35] The dancer *is* the dance! As we saw earlier, Dogen calls fully manifesting ultimate reality "genjokoan," which is none other than our daily, ordinary deportment, rolling up the curtain or getting down from a platform, making a cup of tea or answering the telephone. This is all the manifestation of ultimate reality. We do it everyday.

---

[35]   Yeats, "Among School Children."

Traps and snares can never reach it.

We try so hard to grasp it, to understand it. We try to seize it, to get it, to make sense of its elusive and contradictory nature and somehow put it in a context that we can understand. Our mind creates concepts and ideas about it, but these are nothing but puffs of air, bits of stale bread and dead fish. Try as we might to grasp it with our discursive mind, we will never be able to do so. All we can do is create concepts about it but our discursive, rational and analytical mind can never reach it. It is ungraspable, inconceivable, unrecognizable and far beyond any idea we might have about it.

Once its heart is grasped, you are like the dragon when he gains the water, like the tiger when she enters the mountain.

Seeing our true nature is like coming home to a place that we have never been before but is immediately familiar, comforting and freeing. It's as if we knew this home were there all along even though we had never been there before. And here, at last, we are truly home, and this feeling manifests in a sense of gratitude and freedom to a degree that we may not have ever experienced before. When the dragon gains the water, he is truly home and moves freely. When the tiger enters the mountain, she is where she is most comfortable and moves with a prowess and liberty unequaled anywhere else. This is liberation. Far from being a concept or an idea created by our analytical mind, it is now a living, breathing entity, well beyond the reach of any traps or snares.

For you must know that just there (in zazen) the right Dharma is manifesting itself and that, from the first, dullness and distraction are struck aside.

The right Dharma, as mentioned here, is not opposed to a wrong Dharma. We could also say true Dharma, supreme Dharma, supreme law or perhaps even just the word Dharma all by itself. What need is there for an adjective? This is the world of phenomena just as it is without our interpreting, processing, labeling, evaluating or judging. It is without our creation of a past or a future. It is not enough to simply sit on a cushion, cross our legs and put our hands in some special mudra. We could teach a monkey to do that, or a dog. This is being whereby we are present and conscious of what is going on all around us, including what is going on inside of us. In fact, such phrases as "all around us" or "inside of us" are unnecessary in the sense that there is no inside and no outside. Thoughts arise, pass and dissipate. Our senses detect movement, sounds, colors, odors and feelings. All of this, swirling about in a forever-changing sphere is suchness, just as it is. What is more fascinating than this moment? How could this be dull? How could we be distracted? If there is dullness or distraction in our meditation we might do well by examining our zazen.

When you arise from sitting, move slowly and quietly, calmly and deliberately. Do not rise suddenly or abruptly.

When a period of zazen finishes I don't have any desire to move quickly. There is no need for sharp movements or, for that matter, any talking. It is best to move in accord with those around us and to slowly unfold our legs with the others who are doing the same. If there is a teacher in the room everyone should follow her or his movements and only rise once she or he has begun to rise. This movement after zazen is itself an extension of zazen. There is no need to be in a hurry. One can continue to follow one's breath as one stands up. Zazen continues, therefore, from a sitting posture to a standing one and eventually to walking.

In surveying the past, we find that transcendence of both unenlightenment and enlightenment, and dying while either sitting or standing, have all depended entirely on the strength (of zazen).

Transcendence of unenlightenment is the realization of our true nature. This is what is often referred to as enlightenment. Transcendence of unenlightenment is one's enlightenment to the oneness of all phenomena. From a limited, dualistic perspective entrenched in a lifetime of experience of separation, we suddenly realize that everything is one, that there is no separation whatsoever between the myriad phenomena. Dogen sometimes refers to this as dropped off body and mind.

Although the reality of oneness is now clear to us – to one degree or another – what we fail to see, at least initially, is that this oneness is also empty. What needs to take place is the transcendence of enlightenment, and this transcendence of enlightenment is the realization of the emptiness of the absolute.

The reason that we must transcend enlightenment is that, without realizing it, we have traded one delusion for another, swapping the relative for the absolute. Now, instead of standing on the ground of the relative, we are standing on the ground of the absolute. We have made something out of our enlightenment, we have made something out of the absolute. As crazy as it sounds, our feet are now firmly planted on emptiness. Although we may have transcended unenlightenment, we have not yet transcended our own enlightenment. Enlightenment is not the end of the story. In many ways it's just the beginning. As mentioned earlier, in "The Identity of Relative and Absolute" we chant, "encountering the absolute is not yet enlightenment," which points directly to what Dogen is saying here. Having a great enlightenment experience may be the transcendence of one's delusion about the nature of the relative, but it is not yet the transcendence of one's delusion about the nature of the absolute. How could it be? If transcending unenlightenment is "dropped off body mind," then transcending enlightenment is "dropping off dropped off body mind."

Seeing the absolute clearly may suddenly occur after many years of hard work: sitting zazen, attending retreats, working on koans, meeting with a teacher and endeavoring to clarify the Great Matter with all our heart. Enlightenment can occur at anytime day or night and under any circumstances. It is sudden and comes when we least expect it. It cannot be forecast nor can it be predicted. It can come when we are sitting or when we are walking. This is what Dogen means by "dying while either sitting or standing." This is not the death of the physical body. Of course that can happen at any time as well, but this is what is commonly referred to in Zen parlance as The Great Death. This is not the death of our actual body but rather the death of the limited self that only sees the relative. Of course, that doesn't really die either. There is simply the realization that it's empty. The Buddha, talking about this very subject, referred to the small and limited self as a house builder when he said, "House builder, you have been seen through." The small and limited self has been seen through in the sense that it has been seen as empty, without a solid center. We realize that there is no one inside of ourselves. As we sometimes jokingly say in English, "the lights are on but nobody's home." It's empty. We're empty! And seeing the emptiness of the self, we see the emptiness of all phenomena. This is what Dogen was referring to when he spoke of transcending unenlightenment. So this transcendence of unenlightenment and the further transcendence of enlightenment depends upon our whole-hearted practice of the way, our deep desire to clarify the Great Matter of life and death. We could have great realization, great enlightenment, seeing the oneness of the universe, but if we do not continue on the path, practicing, clarifying and deepening our understanding, whatever experience we have had will only be a memory, fading away with the passage of time. As we have seen earlier, however, the actual experience may occur at anytime, regardless of whether or not we practice zazen. The depth and clarity of that experience, on the other hand, may very well indeed correlate to the depth and power of concentration that we have cultivated through our sitting practice. This is what Master Dogen means when he says that it depends entirely on the strength of our zazen.

In addition, the bringing about of enlightenment by the opportunity provided by a finger, a banner, a needle, or a mallet, and the effecting of realization with the aid of a hossu, a fist, a staff, or a shout, cannot be fully understood by discriminative thinking.

Try as it might, our analytical and discursive mind cannot understand enlightenment, let alone understand how a skillful master might help her or his student with the aid of something so apparently random as a banner, a staff or a shout. How on earth could these things help someone to realize his or her true nature? Master Dogen lists several aids here: a finger, a banner, a needle, a mallet, a hossu, a fist, a staff and a shout. All of these come from famous case koans with which Dogen was intimately familiar having done koan study for many years at Kenninji temple in Kyoto. Take, for example, the finger. This refers to case number three of the *Mumonkan*, also known as *The Gateless Gate*. The *Mumonkan* is a collection of 48 koans compiled in the 13th century by Chinese Zen Master Mumon (1183 – 1260) and published by him when he was 46 years old. It is based on a series of talks that he gave at his temple in China. Case three of the *Mumonkan* is known as "Gutei Raises a Finger." Master Gutei lived in 9th century China and was famous for simply raising a finger whenever he was questioned about Zen. At his temple he had an attendant, and one day a visitor asked the attendant about his master's teaching. The attendant held up a finger. When Gutei heard about this he summoned his attendant to his quarters and promptly chopped off his attendant's finger. As the attendant ran away screaming in pain Gutei called to him. The attendant stopped and looked back. Gutei raised a finger. At this, his attendant was enlightened. This is the entire koan, and a Zen student who is undergoing rigorous training with a master must present this koan in private interview. What is it that this koan is inviting us to see?

This is just one example of the many koans that Dogen cites in the *Fukanzazengi*.[36] In this case, he uses Gutei's Finger and other koans as an illustration of how Zen

---

[36] Tenshin Roshi has said that Maezumi Roshi found 18 references to koans in the *Fukanzazengi* and that he himself was able to find perhaps as many as 21.

masters may help their students have an opening. Of course, this may be an extreme example, but it is indicative of the methods and motives of Zen masters the world over. Our discriminating mind will never understand it.

Indeed, it cannot be fully known by the practicing or realizing of supernatural powers, either.

The realization of one's true nature has nothing whatsoever to do with any sort of psychic ability, the foretelling of the future or the seeing into past lives – nor, for that matter, with any other supernatural powers. There are those who practice meditation in order to cultivate such powers and hone their ability to employ the supernatural, but that is not the aim nor the goal of zazen as practiced in our tradition. There was a time in my own practice when I enjoyed cultivating such powers. I remember once I was on a two-week retreat and I was seated next to someone who seemed to be having a difficult time, so I asked if they would like me to send them some positive energy. The person replied yes, and so during the next period of zazen I sent all the energy I could, and by the end of the period of zazen this person was crying, tears running down their cheeks. During the outside walking meditation before the following period of zazen I asked if everything was alright and they replied yes, saying that it was the most intimate encounter they had ever had with another person. There was something inappropriate in all this and I decided never to use this power again in such a wanton manner. These powers, as impressive and insightful though they may be, cannot compare with realizing one's true nature. We could even say that they have nothing whatsoever to do with one another. The cultivation or dalliance of such powers is merely a distraction or ill-founded detour from the single-minded determination to experience that which Zen masters have been talking about for thousands of years. These distractions are many, and they mainly serve to entertain the discursive mind, but on the road to self discovery they are merely hindrances and should be dealt with as such.

It must be deportment beyond hearing and seeing – is it not a principle that is prior to knowledge and perceptions?

Before we know anything, what is there? Before a single word of philosophy or religion is written down, what is it? Before a single thought, what is this? We know so much. Science has discovered so many laws and philosophy has given us treatises and texts on the human condition along with rich novels that show us how we are as social beings. But before all that, what is there? Before there is a past, before there is a future and even before there is a present, what is it? Now tell me, what is it that is beyond hearing and seeing? What is the one principle that is prior to all knowledge and perceptions? If you can answer these questions you will have repaid all the hard work of the masters of the past and present.

This being the case, intelligence or lack of it does not matter: between the dull and the sharp-witted there is no distinction.

Enlightenment does not depend upon nor rely upon thought or thinking. There is no figuring out enlightenment. As we have seen, our analytical mind cannot touch or grasp it no matter how hard it tries. Our cognitive ability is useless in the quest for our true nature. Obsessed though we may be with intelligence, a high IQ, university education, master's degrees, PhDs or MDs, none of these are of any help to us when we find ourselves on the Way. Intelligence does not matter. Intelligence makes no difference at all. The story of the sixth patriarch, Huineng, as we have already seen, exemplifies this point: he was an illiterate lumberjack who came to realization upon hearing the words of the Diamond Sutra and had a further enlightenment experience with the Fifth Patriarch. On the Way there is no difference between those of low intelligence and high intelligence.

If you concentrate your effort single-mindedly, that in itself is negotiating the Way.

Leaving our intelligence, or lack thereof, aside, all we have to do is practice with all of our heart. This sincere practice immediately brings us into the company of all the great Zen practitioners of the past and those, too, of the present. When we throw our whole heart into our practice, we are aided by all those who have practiced before us and those who are practicing right now. We do not practice alone and this single-minded practice is itself the Way.

Practice-realization is naturally undefiled.

Earlier we saw that Master Dogen considers zazen not only to be the pathway or entrance to enlightenment, but also to be enlightenment itself. This is "practice-realization" which is the manifestation of our true nature which is naturally undefiled. Defiled or undefiled is not based on some moral code of ethics with regards to good or bad, but rather by any conception of duality – or, for that matter, of oneness. A single thought of duality (or oneness) and we are lost. The practice-realization of zazen is beyond duality and oneness and is therefore, naturally, undefiled.

Going forward (in practice) is a matter of everydayness.

Going forward in our practice occurs right here and right now. This sense of "going forward" is nothing more than being natural at this very moment. Being ourselves. Our everyday life is replete with opportunity for deepening our practice without going off and searching for something special, something spiritual or something extraordinary. Going forward is nothing more than the cessation of searching outside of ourselves for the Dharma. This very life, at this very moment, contains everything we could ever want. And this "everydayness" is nothing other than our ordinary, everyday life as it presents itself at this very moment. How could it be otherwise? Our mind is off in its self-created future making plans, or wallowing in its self-created past ruminating over missed opportunities. These fabrications keep it busy and occupied in a daydream of what might be in the future or what could have been in the past, anything except what is right now. This ordinary moment of right now is the same ordinary moment of Shakyamuni Buddha.

Master Rinzai said, "No effort is necessary. You only have to be ordinary with nothing to do – defecating, urinating, wearing clothes, eating food and lying down when tired."[37] Deepening our practice is nothing more than living our life and observing our self in all its manifestations. Our practice does not exist apart from ourselves so wherever we are, whatever we are doing, that is practice. This everydayness is all that there is and this is our practice. What else could there be?

In general, this world, and other worlds as well, both in India and China, equally hold the Buddha-seal, and over all prevails the character of this school, which is simply devotion to sitting, total engagement in immobile sitting.

Dogen wrote this in 1227, long before Buddhism spread to the West. Today, the "Buddha-seal" is all over the world, including the West. I recently attended a public

---

[37] Rinzai, p. 11-12.

lecture by the two people in charge of the Soto Zen School in Europe and they said that zazen is basically dead in the Soto School in Japan. One of them, born and raised in a Soto Zen temple, said that his father – the Abbot of the temple – never even practiced zazen. No one at his temple or in neighboring Soto Zen temples practiced any form of meditation whatsoever. Today the practice of Zen meditation is thriving throughout North America and across Europe where it is practiced daily by thousands of people. How is it in India and China today? I don't know. But here it is in the West and we are slowly adapting Zen practice to our culture and way of life.

Although it is said that there are as many minds as there are persons, still they all negotiate the way solely in zazen.

Dogen emphasizes his strong recommendation of zazen for all people. Each of us has our own unique mind, and yet each of us follows the way through sitting and the study of our mind. The practice-realization of zazen is manifest in the practice and realization of each one of us. In its narrowest interpretation, zazen is sitting meditation, however in a broader and more expansive view, zazen applies to any activity at any moment. Our day-to-day activity is zazen, and it is this everyday activity with which we negotiate the Way. In fact, it is no other than the very Way itself.

Why leave behind the seat that exists in your home and go aimlessly off to the dusty realms of other lands?

Why do we wander here and there looking for the Truth when we can find it right here, wherever we are? In one sense, Dogen, in a rhetorical plea to encourage us from looking outside of ourselves for answers, suggests staying home and sitting on our own cushion instead of aimlessly wandering from one guru to another, from the latest book on Zen to the next one that comes along. In a broader sense, what he's saying here is to take a step backward and turn the light inwards to illuminate the self as Master Rinzai suggests. This "home" that he is talking about is us. This "home" is none other than ourselves, right now, wherever we are, whatever we're doing. Going off aimlessly to the dusty realms of other lands is our penchant for looking outside of ourselves for the Truth. Our lack of faith in our own abilities and our lack of confidence in that which we are capable leads us to follow the words and ideas of those around us or that which we find in books, sutras, films or lectures. Master Rinzai reminds us, "Unwilling to believe in what you have in your own house, you do nothing but seek outside and go clambering after the worthless sayings of the men of old." Our own house is overflowing with riches, yet not realizing this we seek outside. "Don't be taken in by the deluded views of others," says Rinzai, and later he comments, "You seize upon words from the mouths of the old masters and take them to be the True Way. Blind idiots!"[38] Everything we could ever need is right here at our disposal in great abundance so why do we wander off to distant lands like poor mendicants? Why do we seek outside of ourselves for the Truth? Our true nature is right here and there is nowhere that it is not.

If you make one misstep, you go astray from the Way directly before you.

The Way is directly in front of us – in fact, it *is* us! Wherever we are, there's the Way. Yet we seek elsewhere, looking at this one and that one, believing that this phrase or that one will hold the secrets of ultimate Truth. One thought of secular or divine and we are lost! One misstep and we fall into a pit of fire. What is *this*? What is *this*?

You have gained the pivotal opportunity of human form. Do not use your time in vain.

It is considered that human beings are unique in the sense that we can realize our true nature, compared to the sky, a cow or a fence post. Of course, ultimately, we don't know anything, not even this, but our delusion allows us to have this awakening experience. And again, Dogen implores us not to waste our time. Our life is short and the years quickly pass. We have this opportunity right now here on earth so why not take advantage of it?

---

[38] Rinzai, p. 16-17.

You are maintaining the essential working of the Buddha-Way. Who would take wasteful delight in the spark from the flintstone?

Our Zen practice continues and maintains the Zen practice that has been done for thousands of years. In a way, we are the current holders of that practice and it is up to us to maintain it and adapt it to our current needs, just as it has been maintained and adapted from country to country up to the present. Because each one of us has the potential to awaken to our true nature, to waste our lives chasing after fame or riches would be a tragedy. The spark from a flintstone, in and of itself, does little. But if that spark catches fire, it can save our life. Our lives are the spark from the flintstone, as brilliant and ephemeral as a shooting star on a dark night. We can, in this lifetime, ignite a glowing fire that can be seen for miles, a fire that can provide warmth and clarity to others on the Way. Let us not take wasteful delight in our brief lives.

Besides, form and substance are like the dew on the grass, destiny like the dart of lightning – emptied in an instant, vanished in a flash.

The dew of the grass forms overnight and then quickly disappears in the warmth of the morning sun. Form and substance are always changing and so too do our bodies. We were all born and soon we will all die. And just as the dewdrop appears on a blade of grass, so we appear on this earth, and just as a dew drop quickly evaporates in the warmth of the sun, so, too, do we quickly pass away. Our lives are like a bolt of lighting, bright and shinning, illuminating the sky and then suddenly gone. This is how it is with all such phenomena, appearing and disappearing, arising and falling, coming and going, existing and not existing, here one moment and then suddenly gone in a flash.

Please, honored followers of Zen, long accustomed to groping for the elephant, do not be suspicious of the true dragon.

Here, adopting a softer tone, Dogen politely appeals to us to not be afraid of the true dragon. The story of the true dragon dates back to ancient China where there was a man named Seiko who loved dragons. Seiko decorated his house with figures and scrolls depicting different types of dragons and outside in his yard he had dragon figures of various sizes and shapes. Even Seiko's house was built to resemble a dragon. Imagine his love of dragons! Then, one day, a dragon was flying along through the sky near Seiko's house. The dragon saw the house in the form of a dragon and went in for a closer look. Then he saw all the dragon figures out in the yard. *"The person who lives here must love dragons!"* said the dragon to himself. *"I think I'll go down and say hello."* So the dragon swooped down and landed at the front door of Seiko's house. The dragon knocked on the door and when Seiko opened it and saw the dragon he let out a shriek of fright and ran out the back door. The dragon stood there puzzled.

We may be searching for our true nature, but are we truly interested in realizing it? What fears do we have about enlightenment? We fill our houses with objects and representations of what we might think it looks like or should look like, but are we really looking for it and what if we should find it? Dogen, in a gentle admonishment of so many Zen practitioners, says that we are like blind people groping for the elephant. One blind person grabs the elephant's ear and says that the elephant is like a huge palm frond. Another blind person touches the elephant's side and says an elephant is like the wall of a barn. Another blind person grabs the tail and says that the elephant is like a rope. Of course, an elephant is not any of these things – it is so much more. And yet how do we, as Zen practitioners, grasp at our practice and say that Zen is like this or like that or that we should do this or do that? An awakened person should be like this and shouldn't do that, or when I achieve awakening I will have this state of mind or that state of mind. We are like blind people groping for the elephant, thinking that we know what Zen is or what enlightenment is. Let us not be afraid of the *true* dragon.

Devote your energies to a way that directly indicates the absolute.

Master Dogen tells us in no uncertain terms to practice in such a way so as to realize our true nature. Devotion of our energy toward this is most important. Trying to grasp the Way with our mind or figure out what enlightenment is with our intellect is useless. It is, as is often said in Zen, like a gnat trying to bite a bronze bell or like trying to catch a carp with a smooth gourd. Try as we might, we cannot do it. Our discursive mind cannot grasp that which is ungraspable, nor can it understand that which is incomprehensible. Furthermore, seeking enlightenment by studying sutras, books or the words of old masters is pointless. As Master Rinzai said, "[...] attempting to grasp the Buddhadharma through written words [you are] as far away as heaven from earth."[39] Just sit with devotion that one day you will suddenly wake up and realize just *this*.

Revere the person of complete attainment who is beyond all human agency.

In other words, Master Dogen is telling us to find a good teacher. Although we may think that we can navigate the Way alone, either in the solitude of our own home or high on a peak in the mountains, at some point we need guidance and an exchange with another person in order to deepen and clarify our understanding. Experiencing the absolute can happen to anyone, anywhere and of any religion or of no religion. Which path we take to clarify our understanding and deepen our practice will depend, ultimately, on our karma. Some will continue with the Christian or Jewish traditions, others may study Yoga or Buddhism. What is important, according to Dogen, is to find a person whose understanding is clear – and with

---

[39] Rinzai, p. 11.

whom we feel a karmic connection. Someone of "complete attainment" is someone who has realized his or her true nature and is as comfortable with the absolute perspective as he or she is in the relative perspective and who sees the emptiness of both. In other words, someone who simply *is*.

Being "beyond human agency" is sometimes translated as "having nothing more to do," or "beyond study and without intention." Master Rinzai himself said, "Even if you should master a hundred sutras and sastras, you're not as good as a teacher with nothing to do."[40] Find a teacher who has no agenda. Find a teacher who isn't trying to do anything. Find a teacher who has traveled over the terrain and is familiar with it. He or she will have an intimate knowledge of the deep valleys and the high peaks of the journey. He or she will have struggled through the mire of the muddy fields and suffered under the blazing sun. He or she will know the rains of spring and the snows of winter, the pitfalls, the traps and the snares in the forest, the gentle plains and the rolling hills. This teacher has nothing whatsoever to teach.

Gain accord with the enlightenment of the buddhas; succeed to the legitimate lineage of the ancestors' samadhi.

Master Dogen is saying that the awakening experience of Siddhartha Gautama is available to each one of us. This is "gaining accord with the enlightenment of the buddhas."

---

[40] Rinzai, p. 31.

It is not reserved for people who possess a special gift. We, too, can awaken to our true nature just as the Buddha and countless other people have done. Dogen is telling us here to keep going, to go deeper, to awaken to our original face just as the masters of old have done. We must have faith in ourselves and in our own abilities to awaken to the absolute, to be the absolute and to see through the absolute to where there is nothing whatsoever anywhere. This is what Dogen is urging us to do – not just to awaken to our true nature, but to fully penetrate the Great Matter, to go beyond just encountering the absolute. He wants us not only to transcend unenlightenment but also to transcend the transcending – to go beyond and see through our own enlightenment, to have realization within realization, to see clearly the emptiness of emptiness. This is succeeding to the legitimate lineage of the ancestors' samadhi.

Constantly perform in such a manner and you are assured of being a person such as they.

Being a person such as they means to be awakened, to have had a clear realization of enlightenment, to have seen through that enlightenment and to actualize this experience in our everyday life, moment by moment. Dogen reaffirms the possibility of our own awakening if we simply devote ourselves to wholehearted practice of the Way. This is "constantly perform in such a manner," which means that our practice is never ending. It's something that we must do constantly all day long, everyday. As we have seen previously, Zen Master Hakuin's teacher, Master Shoju, referred to this as "continuous and unremitting devotion" to practice. "This means immersing yourself totally in your practice at all times and in all your daily activities – walking, standing, sitting or lying down."[41] This is what Master Dogen means by constantly performing in such a manner as they: thoroughly engaging in this never-ending practice of actualizing our understanding at this very moment, now and forever in the endless unfolding thusness of our lives.

Your treasure-store will open of itself, and you will use it at will.

The opening of our treasure-store is the realization of our true nature and the manifestation of it in our life. It's the realization of *just this*. We can all realize this gift in our lifetime through the diligent, wholehearted practice of the Way. No one else can do it for us. Nevertheless, it opens of itself, as a gift arriving unexpectedly. When this happens we see that we have gained nothing and that this treasure-store has been with us all along. In fact, it is everywhere.

Having invited us to gain accord with the enlightenment of the Buddhas, Master Dogen encourages us to see the emptiness of emptiness, to have realization within realization, to drop off this dropping off of body and

---

[41] Waddell, *Wild Ivy*, pp. 34-35.

mind and to have the experience of enlightenment pulled out from beneath us until there is nowhere for us to stand, no solid ground anywhere for us to walk upon. Having seen through the relative and experienced our true nature, Dogen wants us to go further and see through the absolute until there is nothing whatsoever anywhere – nothing, nothing, nothing. Not even this nothing. This is what Master Dogen calls transcending enlightenment.

Now our treasure-store is illuminated with the unfathomable and exquisite light of our whole being and wherever we may find ourselves we give freely of this most precious gift, using it at will, wielding it skillfully, mercifully and implacably. This is what Master Dogen was referring to when he spoke about the perfection and all-pervasiveness of the Way. This is our practice and this is our life, continuing endlessly and forever, far beyond the reaches of our vision.

Acknowledgements

I would like to thank Rev. Charles Tenshin Fletcher Roshi, abbott of Yokoji Zen Mountain Center in California, for his invitation to study the *Fukanzazengi* over the course of the 2018 Spring Training Period. Tenshin Roshi encouraged me to go deeper into my meditation practice and never allowed me to become complacent in my understanding.

I would also like to thank Rev. Dr. David Keizan Scott Roshi of the StoneWater Zen Sangha in Liverpool, England, for his enthusiasm for this commentary and also for having invited me to give several public talks on it. His students and their questions helped me to articulate more precisely what I see in Dogen's writing.

Rev. Catherine Genno Pagès Roshi of Dana Sangha in Montreuil, France, was a supportive reader and gave me thoughtful advice for which I am most grateful.

Dr. Amy Laine was a great support while I was working on this text in Cambridge, Massachusetts as was Rev. Dr. Jo O'Riorden while I was writing for many months in Liverpool, England.

Grateful acknowledgement is given to The Eastern Buddhist Society in Kyoto, Japan, for permission to reprint Norman Waddell and Abe Masao's translation of the *Fukanzazengi*, which first appeared in the journal, "The Eastern Buddhist," Vol. 6, No. 2 in October, 1973.

Works Cited

Bielefeldt, Carl. "Ch'ang-lu Tsung-tse's *Tso-Ch'an I* and the 'Secret' of Zen Meditation." Ed. Peter N Gregory. *Traditions of Meditation in Chinese Buddhism*. University of Hawai'i Press, 1986.

Bielefeldt, Carl. *Dogen's Manuals of Zen Meditation*. University of California Press, 1988.

Dogen, Eihei. *The Wholehearted Way*. Kosho Uchiyama, commentary. Shokaku Okumura and Taigen Daniel Leighton, translators. Tuttle Publishing, 1977.

Dogen, Eihei. "Dogen's 'Bendowa.'" Norman Waddell and Abe Masao, translators. "The Eastern Buddhist," New Series, Vol. 4, No. 1 (May, 1971), pp. 124-127.

Dogen, Eihei. "Fukanzazengi." Norman Waddell and Abe Masao, translators. "The Eastern Buddhist," New Series, Vol. 6, No. 2 (October, 1973), pp. 115-128.

Kapleau, Philip, ed. *The Three Pillars of Zen: Teaching, Practice and Enlightenment.* Beacon Press, 1967.

Leighton, Taigen Dan, ed. *Dogen's Extensive Record: A Translation of the Eihei Koroku.* Taigen Dan Leighton and Shohaku Okumura, translators. Wisdom, 2010.

Loori, John Daido. "Dropping off Body and Mind." *Mountain Record.* 21, no. 1, Fall, 2002.

Loori, John Daido and Kazuaki Tanahashi, translators. *The True Dharma Eye: Zen Master Dogen's Three Hundred Koans.* Shambhala, 2011.

Maezumi, Hakuyu Taizan and Glassman, Bernard Tetsugen, eds. *On Zen Practice II.* Zen Center of Los Angeles, 1977.

Merzel, D. Genpo. *Spitting Out The Bones: A Zen Master's 45 Year Journey.* Big Mind Publishing, 2016.

Rinzai. *The Record of Linji.* Thomas Yuho Kirchner, ed. Ruth Fuller Sasaki, translator and commentary. 1975. University of Hawai'i Press, 2009.

Waddell, Norman, translator. *The Essential Teachings of Zen Master Hakuin*. Shambhala, 1994.

Waddell, Norman, translator. *Wild Ivy: The Spiritual Autobiography of Zen Master Hakuin*. Shambhala, 2001.

Waddell, Norman and Masao Abe, translators. *The Heart of Dogen's Shobogenzo*. State University of New York Press, 2002.

Yamada, Kohun. "Dogen Zenji and Enlightenment" in *On Zen Practice II*. Hakuyu Taizan Maezumi and Bernard Tetsugen Glassman, editors. Zen Center of Los Angeles, 1977.

Yampolsky, Philip P., translator. *The Zen Master Hakuin. Selected Writings*. Columbia University Press, 1971.

Yeats, W. B. *The Poems of W.B. Yeats, A New Edition*. Macmillan Publishing Company, 1933.

www.ingramcontent.com/pod-product-compliance
Lightning Source LLC
Chambersburg PA
CBHW020947090426
42736CB00010B/1304